Th
General Edi

IN THE STREETS
OF CALCUTTA

THE STORY OF MOTHER TERESA

Audrey Constant

RELIGIOUS AND MORAL EDUCATION PRESS

Religious and Moral Education Press
An imprint of Chansitor Publications Ltd
A Subsidiary Company of Hymns Ancient & Modern Ltd
St Mary's Works, St Mary's Plain
Norwich, Norfolk NR3 3BH

First published 1980

Reprinted 1981, 1982, 1984, 1989

New Imprint 1992

Reprinted 1993 (twice), 1994

Printed in Great Britain by BPC Wheatons Ltd, Exeter

ISBN 0 900274 68 9

IN THE STREETS OF CALCUTTA

The Story of Mother Teresa

A woman lay dying on a Calcutta pavement. Her feet were half eaten away by rats and ants. She had been lying there for days and no one had taken any notice of her.

Then a nun came along. She was a tiny woman, dressed in a white sari which hung loosely about her and covered her head. She walked quickly, for she was always in a hurry. Her name was Mother Teresa.

When she saw the woman on the pavement she stopped. Full of pity, she picked her up and carried her into a nearby hospital for treatment. They told her there that the woman was too ill and poor to bother about. Besides, they had no room. Mother Teresa pleaded with them, but they said there was nothing they could do for her. However, she would not leave her patient, and set off for another hospital. But it was in vain. The woman died.

This was not the only person Mother Teresa found dying on the streets. There were many of them. There was an old man who was so thin he looked like a child. It was pouring with rain when Mother Teresa found him lying dead under a tree in a mess of sickness and blood. He was outside a hospital but no one had taken him in.

Cats and dogs are treated better than this, thought Mother

Teresa, sadly. She made up her mind that she would find a place where she could care for these people herself. The hospitals would not take them in. There was no one else to look after them. So she would do so herself.

Teacher in India

Mother Teresa was born in Yugoslavia. She was brought up with her brother and sister in a happy Christian home. Her name was Agnes. Ever since she was twelve years old she was quite sure she was going to spend her life serving God.

While she was still at school she heard about some nuns who were working in India. They were called the Loreto nuns, and their special work was teaching. Agnes wanted to go to India herself and work with them. When she was seventeen she asked if she could join the Loreto nuns.

Their headquarters was (and still is) in Ireland, so first she went to Dublin. Soon afterwards she was sent to Darjeeling in India. It must have been very hard for her to leave her home and family, and sail off to a country so far away.

In India she became a novice, which means that she was learning to become a nun. This is not easy, for a nun has to make certain vows or promises. She has to promise to give up life in the outside world and live in a convent. Much of her time is spent in prayer, and she promises never to marry. Since Loreto nuns run schools, she also trained as a teacher.

When Agnes took her final vows and became a nun she was given a new name – Teresa.

From Darjeeling she went to a convent in Calcutta. This convent was in a poor area of the city. It was surrounded by high walls which hid the slums outside. Within the walls, white buildings gleamed under the hot sun and green lawns were shaded by trees.

It was here that Mother Teresa came to teach geography

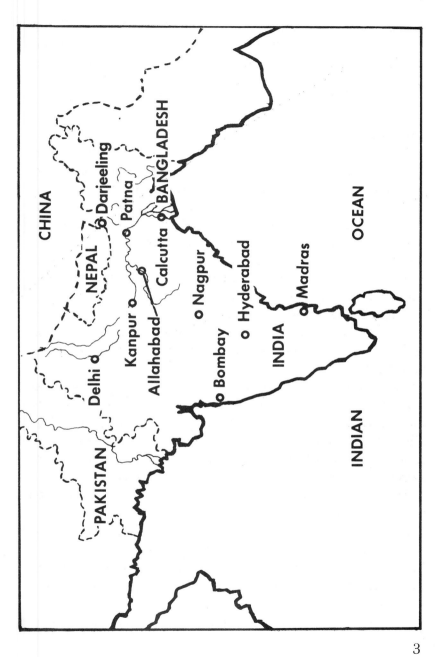

in St Mary's School. Her pupils came from rich families who could afford to have their children educated. They were well behaved and neatly dressed. She found life pleasant in that peaceful place. But outside those walls were people who were sick and hungry. Many of them were homeless.

Many disasters occur in India such as floods and drought. It is then that the crops die and people starve. They leave their villages and come into already overcrowded cities like Calcutta. They think they will find work there. It is a terrible problem to provide food and shelter for so many people. Many people die in the streets. Children and babies are left to starve because their parents cannot provide for them.

One day Mother Teresa had to go into this very poor part of the city. She found people living in rows of huts with mud floors. Others had made shelters out of old wooden boxes and bits of sacking. People wore clothes which were little more than rags. Cows and stray dogs looked for food among the rubbish in the streets. She stepped over people lying on the pavements. Some were too ill even to beg.

When she returned to the convent she could not forget about them. She wanted to be with them and do something to help them.

Mother Teresa must have often thought and prayed about what God wanted her to do. It was not until some time later, when she was on a train going up to the hills, that suddenly she knew the answer. She was to give up her life in the convent and go into the slums to serve the poor. For her it was not enough just to offer prayers to God. She wanted to serve Him by helping these poor people herself. She was certain that this was God's will.

Because of the promises she had made when she joined the Loreto nuns, she had first to ask permission to leave the convent. It was two more years before she was allowed to go.

At last she was free to do the work she was so sure God

4

A typical night-time scene in Calcutta

meant her to do. Up to now she had been a teacher. But if she was to be of any use to those sick people she must learn to nurse. She went to a town called Patna to train with a Nursing Order of Nuns. Then she returned to Calcutta. Alone, and with only a few rupees in her pocket, she set out for the poorest part of the city. Among the dirt and misery she began her work.

A family offered her a room in their house. She moved in with her things – just a suitcase and a chair she had been given. The family refused to take any money for the rent, or for the food and medicines they gave her.

People with every kind of illness came to her to be cured. Soon after she started, one of her patients had to have a poisoned thumb removed. Taking a pair of scissors and saying a prayer Mother Teresa cut it off. Her patient fainted, and so did she! But the man lived. Her first operation was a success.

Mother Teresa went into the slum homes and nursed the sick and dying. It seemed an impossible task she had set herself, but she was not afraid. She was sure that God wanted her to do this work. She knew that if it was only her own idea, the work would fail. But if it was God's work it would live and grow.

Many of the children in the slums had never been to school. So she gathered them together and started one. It was just an open space among the huts. No blackboards, no benches – nothing. The first thing she taught these children was a prayer. Then she told them how to keep themselves clean. She scraped away the grass and, taking a stick, began writing the alphabet on the earth.

The next day someone brought a table, then a chair and later a cupboard. A blackboard followed. To begin with, that was all the furniture she had. Some of the girls Mother Teresa had taught at St Mary's school were now old enough to start work. They came to help her.

A few rich Indian women heard about her work and also

6

Mother Teresa begins her first school

came to help. They brought with them money and medicines, though she had not asked for either. Slowly the school grew, and now there are many more like it.

She took some of the girls to live with her. Soon there were so many that they took over the whole upper floor of the house. Mother Teresa called these girls her Sisters.

Home for the Dying

For five years Mother Teresa and her Sisters tended the sick and dying on the streets. The hospitals were full and there was nowhere else to take them. They even had to beg for medicines to treat their patients.

Mother Teresa took her problem to the city council of Calcutta. She begged the council to give her a place where people could die with someone to love and care for them. "It is a shame for people to die on our city roads," she said.

The health officer showed her a building near the great Hindu temple, Kalighat. He suggested she might use part of it for her purpose. It was once used as a rest-house where Hindus came after they had worshipped their goddess. Now it was used by thugs and layabouts as a place for gambling and drinking.

Mother Teresa knew that most of the city's poor came here to die, as it was a holy place for Hindus. It did not matter to her whether her patients were Hindus, Buddhists, Sikhs or Muslims. She just wanted to show these poor, sick people the love of Jesus. As the Bible says, "When you do it to these my brothers you do it to me." She gladly accepted the building and within twenty-four hours she brought her first patients here.

To begin with she had a bad time. People thought she was using the place to convert the Hindus to Christianity. They threw stones at her and tried to drive her away.

Then one day she saw a crowd on the pavement outside

the temple. In the middle was a man dying in the gutter. He had a dreadful illness called cholera and no one would touch him. Mother Teresa herself picked him up and took him to her Home, where he died peacefully. He had been a priest in the Hindu temple. She had no more trouble after that. People thought that, as she had cared for one of their priests, she must be a good woman.

She called this place Nirmal Hriday, which means "Place of the Pure Heart". Now it is full of people who have been brought in off the streets. Outside it is a plain, ugly building of grey stone. Inside, a soft light shines on the rows of patients as the Sisters move quietly among the sick, feeding and caring for them. It is a very peaceful place.

Mother Teresa and her Sisters have taken in many

Some families make their homes in segments of pipeline

thousands of people off the streets. Half of them die quite soon afterwards, but Mother Teresa is content that they die peacefully. She does not see suffering and death as a sad event. She calls it "Going home".

"What these poor people need even more than food and shelter, is to be wanted," she says. "They understand that even if they have only a few hours left to live, they are loved. However dirty and sick they are, someone cares for them."

Some of the patients do recover, and those that are well enough to work are helped to find jobs.

The Sisters of Charity

In 1950 Mother Teresa's Sisters were formed into an organisation called the Missionaries of Charity. They were so named because they loved and cared for those in need. A Mother House was founded at the same time and this became the headquarters of the Missionaries of Charity.

Mother Teresa now had many people helping her, including doctors and nurses. When people heard about the wonderful work she was doing, they wanted to help. They gave her money to buy food and medicines for her patients.

Although she is glad when young girls want to join her, she always makes sure that they understand what a hard life it will be. It needs courage and unselfishness to look after these poor, helpless people. Many of the girls who join come from rich homes and are quite unused to this sort of work. The training is long and difficult, but Mother Teresa is patient with them. She understands because she, too, was once a novice.

For the first six months the novices watch the Sisters at work and help in small ways. This gives them time to decide if it really is the work for them. They have not yet taken their final vows and there is still time for them to change their minds.

Mother Teresa believes that they can only truly understand and help the poor by being like them. So her Sisters live in

10

Nirmal Hriday—Mother Teresa's first Home for the Dying

Mother Teresa distributing food

the same way as the people they serve. They eat the same food and wear only their simple white saris bordered with blue. They do not have fans to cool the air or use anything to add comfort to their lives. They worship and pray within the sound of roaring traffic. They are taught never to spare themselves.

In spite of the hardships very few of the Sisters want to leave. Their work is their way of showing their love for Christ, and they want to give the best they can. They are naturally joyful because they have found that the secret of happiness lies in helping others.

Today there is medicine to cure all kinds of disease. But being unwanted is the worst thing that can happen to a human being. The Sisters, with their willing hands and loving hearts, can prevent this happening.

The day begins for them at four-thirty in the morning. First they meet for prayers, to draw strength for the day's work ahead of them. Then they have their first meal. They clean the house and do the washing before they go out to work. Each of them has a shining bucket. This and their simple clothes are the only things they own.

In one of the class-rooms a nun is teaching the novices. They listen carefully as she speaks to them. "Let the poor use you. Be kind and merciful. Let no one ever come to you without going away better and happier. Let there be kindness in your face, kindness in your eyes, kindness in your smile, kindness in your warm greeting. . . . In each suffering person you can see Jesus."

The novices also have to pass tests on the kind of work they will do in the schools and clinics.

Meanwhile the Sisters set off for their duties outside the Home. Some go to the Home for the Dying, some to the children's Homes. Others work at leprosy clinics or give out medicines. Hot food is prepared. It is taken out to the streets and given to starving people. Thousands are fed each day.

There are well over two thousand Sisters. They have to be prepared to go wherever they are sent.

For some time Mother Teresa felt that there was a great need for men to help with the work. There were some jobs that they could do better than women, especially with boys and young men. She went to the Archbishop of Calcutta, and in 1963 he blessed the beginnings of a new group, the Missionary Brothers of Charity.

Mother Teresa found just the right person to put in charge of them. He was Father Andrew, a priest who came from Australia.

Now there are over 350 Brothers. They have opened Homes for mentally and physically handicapped people, and run schools, youth centres and health clinics.

Children's Homes

There are more than fifty Homes for children who have no family to look after them. Their parents might have died, or left them because they had no money to buy food.

In these Homes, called Shishu Bhavan, there are babies that have been picked up from the pavements, left on doorsteps or outside police posts. Some have been found in drains or rubbish dumps. Or they might come from hospitals. Mother Teresa has said that she wants all unwanted babies.

There are so many babies in her Homes that they sleep three in a cot, but Mother Teresa always finds a place for more infants. Many of them die, but others, with loving care, survive. Homes are found for nearly all of them. Many go to Indian couples who have no children of their own. Others are adopted by families outside India.

Some of the older children who cannot walk properly go to France to be looked after. The French people asked if they could be allowed to help in this way. This is because they have found a cure for these lame children.

The children for whom no suitable homes can be found stay with Mother Teresa until they marry and have homes of their own. Whatever the reason, Mother Teresa never refuses a child a place. "Somehow there is always one more bed," she says happily.

Caring for people with leprosy

Leprosy is a widespread disease in hot countries. There are over 4 million people in India suffering from it.

It is usually caught by living for a long time with someone who has already got the disease. People are very afraid of catching it. They will sometimes turn a relative out of his own home if they think he has leprosy.

The disease often begins with a loss of feeling when the nerves die. If a sufferer cuts himself he cannot feel it. As a result the cut can easily be poisoned and become a serious wound. This can affect the bones and even lead to loss of limbs.

In other cases lumps form on the sufferer's head, often affecting his nose and ears. This makes him look very ugly. These days, however, leprosy sufferers can be completely cured if treated in time. They are able to lead normal lives and even to work for their own living.

Mother Teresa first started a leprosy clinic about twenty years ago on a piece of land close to the railway lines. It was a dangerous area, and some of the lame people were involved in accidents with the passing trains. But land was hard to find and Mother Teresa was glad to have a place to bring her first five leprosy patients.

Their numbers quickly grew. Then, just when she needed him, a doctor came to her and offered his services. His name was Dr Sen and he was a specialist in leprosy work. He took charge of the clinic and trained Sisters to look after these patients. Now there are 122 leprosy clinics.

15

Many more people could be healed if they understood that they must keep up with the treatment. They leave long gaps without coming to the clinic as, for instance, one man who had been in prison for murder. When the pain was very bad he would come back for a few days. When he felt better he went off to drink. Then he became violent and got into trouble with the police. He had been coming and going like this for twelve years and the Sisters had grown fond of him. He had never been loved before and he could not understand it. He used to say, "You Sisters have defeated me. You love even the wicked."

Most of the people helping in the leprosy clinics are sufferers themselves. They fetch and carry things, and take food to those who are too ill to walk. They have their own church in Calcutta. At Christmas there is a special service which they all like to attend, whatever their religion. Those who cannot move on their own are carried to church by the other sufferers.

Co-workers

Mother Teresa wants to use everyone all over the world who offer to help her. She calls these people her Co-workers – her partners in work. There are thousands of them around the world. They spread the news of her work and help the poor in their own countries.

In Great Britain, as in many other places, groups of Co-workers collect wool and cloth so that elderly or handicapped people can help to make clothing and blankets. Large amounts of clothing, bandages and medicines are sent to India each year.

Not long ago another place was opened in the East End, one of the poorest areas of London. Here there are many homeless people. Each Christmas, Co-workers help the Sisters

16

to give a party for them in the Hall of Westminster Cathedral. After the meal they all sing carols.

In 1977 a young lad of seventeen set off to sail alone across the Atlantic. He succeeded and, through his sponsors, raised a lot of money which he sent to Mother Teresa.

A woman in Austria has knitted and sewn hundreds of children's clothes. She bought all the wool and material herself. Another woman has brought an eighty-one-year-old man into her home and looks after him. A young widow with two children of her own has taken four homeless children to live with her.

In Australia a man called Paul Smith has opened a Home for men who are trying to give up drink. His friends who also wanted to help bought all the mattresses for the Home. In Germany two girls told their parents they wanted to do without new dresses and, instead, asked that the money be sent to Mother Teresa.

In Switzerland a woman gave all her family jewels to Mother Teresa. The sale of these just covered the amount needed to buy fifty-two beds for a new leprosy clinic in Calcutta. From Malta, parties of young people go to Sicily during their holidays to help the Sisters there. Others visit Naples to work in the slums. Young Co-workers go to India and other Third World countries to work in Mother Teresa's Homes.

There are many sick, lonely people in the world, people who live alone or have no friends or relatives. Mother Teresa needs the help of these people especially. She believes that through their prayers her work will grow. They, in their turn, feel they belong to Mother Teresa's family.

The work spreads

At first Mother Teresa worked only in India, but then gradually people all over the world began to hear about her. They wanted her to come to their countries as well.

A bishop in South America asked her to do the same work

for the poor in Venezuela. The Pope asked her to come to the slums of Rome. Later the work spread to Tanzania, Mauritius, the Yemen, Jordan, Australia and Peru. The Missionaries of Charity now work in most countries of the world.

Whenever there is a disaster, Mother Teresa goes there herself to help. She went to Andhra Pradesh, in south-east India, when it was hit by a terrible storm. A tidal wave, 18 feet high, swept inland for 15 miles and destroyed a whole village. She and her Sisters worked round the clock, feeding and clothing an endless stream of people who had lost everything.

Some people think that such a big task is beyond a small band of people. They say it should be done by the Government. But Mother Teresa says, "In Christ we can do all things. That's why our work is possible. Without Him we can do nothing." She goes on, "We feel that what we are doing is just a drop in the ocean. But if that drop was not in the ocean, I think the ocean would be less because of that missing drop."

These days everyone is in a hurry. In the rush, some people get left behind. Unlike Mother Teresa and her Sisters, many of us are too busy to bother much about them. We have enough to eat and people who love us. We often forget about the people in other parts of the world who are hungry and sick and have nowhere to live.

Many children are interested in Mother Teresa's work and want to help. Some of them go without something they want, or save their pocket-money to send to Mother Teresa.

She likes to tell the children what she is using it for. For example, money sent by children in Britain goes to buy flour to make bread. A daily slice is given to starving Indian children. The money sent by children from Denmark buys milk. German children provide the money for vitamin tablets. These are wonderful ways of showing love and concern.

18

Mother Teresa with a rescued baby

Nirmal Hriday Silver Jubilee Year

The year 1977 was a very special year in Calcutta. Twenty-five years had passed since Mother Teresa had brought her first patients to Nirmal Hriday. She wanted to make it a time to remember.

Some of the richest people in the world live in India, but there are millions who are poor. Mother Teresa wanted the two kinds of people to meet, so she invited the rich to visit her Homes in Calcutta. She wanted them to see for themselves what it was like to have nothing. In doing so she hoped they would care about the poor.

The rich people came in great numbers. They all wanted to join in this wonderful idea. It lasted for four days and people gave as much as they could. All the Homes were visited.

In recent years Mother Teresa has formed more branches of the Missionaries of Charity. In 1977 she founded a contemplative branch in New York, called the Sisters of the Word. It is an enclosed order whose purpose is to link and support the Missionaries of Charity through prayer. In 1978 a similar order, the Brothers of Charity, was formed in Rome, and in 1984 Mother Teresa founded the Missionaries of Charity Fathers. Their ministry in the Church is threefold: 1. Priestly service to the poorest of the poor on a person-to-person basis. 2. Sharing with brother priests a deeper prayer life, poverty and charity. 3. Providing spiritual assistance to the entire Missionaries of Charity Family.

Mother Teresa's family give help all over the world in many ways. Here are some of them:

Schools

Homes for the destitute
  dying

Children's homes

Welfare clinics

Help for drug addicts

Care of AIDS sufferers

Soup kitchens

Soup runs for homeless people
  sleeping out

Travelling clinics	Family visiting
Leprosy clinics	Hospital visiting
Dispensaries	Prison visiting

Mother Teresa often has to travel all over the world to visit her Sisters and Co-workers. But wherever she goes, she always longs to be back in Calcutta with her poor.

This is her prayer:

> Make us worthy, Lord to serve our fellow men throughout the world who live and die poor and hungry. Give them, through our hands, this day their daily bread. By our understanding love, give them Peace and Joy.

BIOGRAPHICAL NOTES'

Mother Teresa was born in Yugoslavia on 27 August 1910. She went to a government school and while there she heard about a Teaching Order of Nuns working in Calcutta. She applied to join the Order.

In November 1928 she was sent to Loreto Abbey in Dublin, and from there to Darjeeling in India. From 1929 to 1948 she taught geography at St Mary's High School in Calcutta. For some years she was principal of the school.

10 September 1946 was her "Day of Decision". Mother Teresa asked for permission from her Superior to live alone outside the convent and to work in the Calcutta slums. Her request was sent to the Pope in Rome and approved. In August 1948 she went to Patna for three months to the American Medical Missionary Sisters for nursing training. By Christmas she was back in Calcutta.

December 1948 She opened her first slum school.

March 1949 Her first helper arrived, a young Bengali girl.

October 1950 The Congregation of the Missionaries of Charity was approved and instituted in Calcutta and from there spread throughout India.

March 1963 The Archbishop of Calcutta blessed the beginnings of a new branch, the Missionary Brothers of Charity.

In 1965 An international appeal was made which resulted in gifts of money. The work now spread across the world. Centres were also opened to train novices.

In 1983 there were over two hundred Houses of Missionaries of Charity, in 52 countries. In Britain, there were Houses in the London area, Dublin, Liverpool and Livingston.

Mother Teresa has received many awards. Here is a list of some of them:

January 1971 The Pope John XXIII Peace Prize awarded by Pope Paul VI.

September 1971 The Good Samaritan Award in Boston, U.S.A.

October 1971 The John F. Kennedy International Award.

November 1972 The Jawaharlal Nehru Award for International Understanding awarded by the Indian Government.

April 1973 The Templeton Award for "Progress in Religion" presented by Prince Philip.

October 1975 The Albert Schweitzer International Prize.

1977 Sisters of the Word, a contemplative branch of Missionaries of Charity founded in New York.

June 1977 Honorary degree of Doctor of Divinity, bestowed by Prince Philip at Cambridge University.

1978 Brothers of the Word formed in Rome.

July 1978 Order of the British Empire presented by the Australian High Commissioner in Delhi.

October 1979 Awarded the Nobel Peace Prize.

November 1983 Order of Merit presented in India by the Queen.

1984 Missionaries of Charity Fathers founded.

THINGS TO DO

A Test yourself

Here are some short questions. See if you can remember the answers from what you have read. Then write them down in a few words.

1 How old was Mother Teresa when she decided to use her life to serve God?
2 What kind of work did she do at first with the Loreto nuns?
3 What was the first operation she carried out?
4 Who brought money and medicine for Mother Teresa's work?
5 How many people have Mother Teresa and her Sisters taken in off the streets?
6 What did she feel the poor people needed even more than food and shelter?
7 Why were men needed to help with the work?
8 Mention some of the places where Mother Teresa found the babies she took in?
9 How did Dr Sen help Mother Teresa?
10 Why was 1977 a special year for Mother Teresa?

B Think through

These questions need longer answers. Think about them, and then try to write two or three sentences in answer to each one. You may look up the story again to help you.

1 Why do people in India leave their villages to live in overcrowded cities like Calcutta?
2 Why did Mother Teresa give up teaching at St Mary's School?
3 Why do the Sisters of the Missionaries of Charity live in the same way as the people they serve?
4 What does the name "Nirmal Hriday" mean? For what purpose did Mother Teresa use this building?
5 What are "Co-workers"? How do they help in the work?
6 In what ways have children from Britain, Denmark and Germany helped Mother Teresa?

C To talk about

Here are some questions for you to discuss together. Try to give reasons for what you say or think. Try to find out the different opinions which people have about each question.

1 Is it true to say that we treat cats and dogs better than we sometimes treat human beings?

2 Why do you think some people are very rich and some people very poor? Would it be fairer if all the wealth in the world was shared equally?

3 Why do you think Mother Teresa started her children's work by opening a school? Is it important that all children should receive an education?

4 Do you think that everyone should die knowing that somebody cares for them? Or do you think it is a waste of time trying to help people who are going to die anyway?

5 Jesus said that there is greater happiness in giving than in receiving. Do you agree? Is it really true that the secret of happiness lies in helping other people in the way Mother Teresa does?

D Find out

Choose one or two of the subjects below and find out all you can about them. History books, geography books and encyclopaedias may be useful. Perhaps you can use reference books in your library to look up some of the names and places.

1 *India*

   (a) Draw the map of India on page 3.

   (b) What is the climate of India like? Why does the country sometimes suffer from drought and famine, and at other times from terrible floods?

   (c) Find out how people live in the villages of India. What crops do they grow?

   (d) Why is the population of India growing so fast? What is the Government trying to do about it?

   (e) Find out about the main towns of India. What are the chief industries?

   (f) What modern developments are taking place in India?

2 *Hinduism*

   Hinduism is the main religion of India.

   (a) Find out about some of the Hindu gods, such as Siva, Vishnu and Shakti. Try to find pictures of them, and some of the stories that are told about them.

24

(b) Draw a picture of a Hindu temple, and find out how such a temple is used.

(c) What is a sadhu? What is a guru? What do they do?

(d) How do Hindus use yoga? What is it supposed to do for people?

3 *Nuns*

(a) Find out about nuns in the Roman Catholic Church. What promises do they make? What different kinds of work do they do?

(b) What can you learn about the Loreto nuns?

(c) Why do girls become nuns?

4 *Relief work*

(a) What is meant by the term the "Third World"?

(b) Find out about *one* other organisation that helps people in need in the Third World – Christian Aid, Oxfam, TEAR Fund, etc.

(c) How can people in this country help the work of the Missionaries of Charity?

5 *Leprosy*

(a) Find out about the disease of leprosy and how it is treated.

(b) Read the story of Father Damien (*Island of No Return*, by Geoffrey Hanks, R.E.P.), and give a short account of his work.

(c) What work does the Leprosy Mission do today?

USEFUL INFORMATION

Addresses

Hon. Secretary
Co-Workers of Mother Teresa
177 Bravington Road
London W9.

TEAR Fund
1 Bridgeman Road
Teddington
Middlesex TW11 9AJ.

Christian Aid
240–250 Ferndale Road
London SW9 8BH.

The Youth Secretary
The Leprosy Mission
50 Portland Place
London W1N 3DG.

N.B. Remember to enclose a stamped, addressed envelope for the reply.

More books to read

The Church in the Third World, by Ian Birnie, Focus on Christianity series (Edward Arnold) (P).

For Love of God, by George Gorree (Shand Alba Publications) (T).

For the Brotherhood of Man under the Fatherhood of God, by Kathryn Spink (Colour Library International) (P/T).

Mother Teresa, by Sheila Hobden, People with a Purpose series (SCM Press) (P).

Mother Teresa – Her People and Her Work, by Desmond Doig (Collins, Fontana) (T).

Something Beautiful for God, by Malcolm Muggeridge (Collins) (T).

The Third World, by Roger Clare, World Topic series (Macdonald Educational) (P).

(T) = suitable for teachers and older pupils
(P) = suitable for younger pupils

Films

Angel with a Bushy Beard (25 min), colour. Tells the story of a Salvation Army Major working among the poor people of Calcutta. Available from The Salvation Army, 101 Queen Victoria Street, London EC4P 4EP.

India (25 min), colour. An excellent background film. Available from the Baptist Missionary Society, 93–97 Gloucester Place, London W1H 4AA.

Films (cont.)

The Living City (30 min), colour. Shows some of the changes taking place in Calcutta. Available from either Christian Aid or Concord Films Council, 201 Felixstowe Road, Ipswich, Suffolk IP3 9BJ.

Mother Teresa of Calcutta (15 min), black and white, and *Something Beautiful for God* (50 min), colour. Both available from either Mrs T. Bethell, The Small House, Cliftonville, Dorking, Surrey, *or* Concord Films Council.

Other sources of help

C.E.M. Leaflet No. 20 – *Mother Teresa*, is supplied free of charge, except where large numbers are requested, from C.E.M., Annandale, Chester House, Pages Lane, London N10 1PR.

Information about India may be obtained from The Commonwealth Institute, Kensington High Street, London W8 6NQ.